YOUR CHILD
LEARNS TO CHOOSE

Andrew D. Thompson

ABBEY PRESS
St. Meinrad, Indiana 47577

DEDICATION

To my loving wife Betty, whose gracefulness and intelligence helped bring these thoughts to light. And to Beth and Greg, whose playfulness and development have made it easy to believe in the mystery of each person.

ACKNOWLEDGEMENT

The research on which this brief book is based was supported in part by funds from Boys Town. The conclusions drawn—both in the form of opinions and suggested policies—are those of the author and do not necessarily reflect those of Boys Town.

PHOTO CREDITS: Smith/Garza, Cover; Ron Engh, page 4; Rick Smolan, page 8; Michael Hayman/Image, page 17; David Hiebert, page 22; Paul S. Conklin, pages 46, 68, 83, and 90; Ann Leslie, page 56.

Library of Congress Catalog Card Number: 78-73018
ISBN: 0-87029-145-9

©1978 St. Meinrad Archabbey
St. Meinrad, Indiana 47577

241.9
THO

CONTENTS

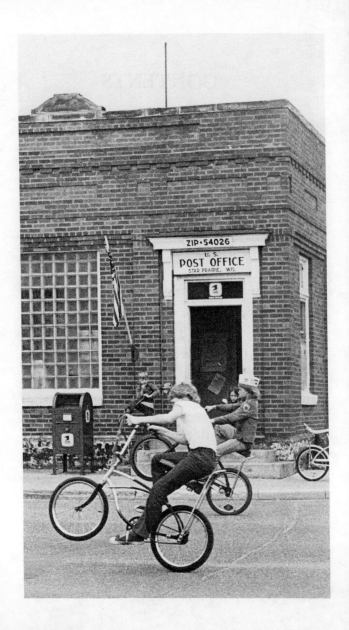

FOREWORD

Shifts apparent in the very basic value structure of contemporary society are making a profound difference for parents who want to raise their children to become responsible Christians. Not all the changes appear to be for the better and some parents report considerable frustration. They find that society, even at the neighborhood level, seems less personal and more materialistic than when they were growing up. The schools seem to spend more time on discipline problems and less on teaching a standard content. The churches not only do not look the same physically, but the religious teachings, language, and rituals seem to bespeak new understandings as well. Witnessing such changes, parents might well feel adrift without their traditional, fixed moorings.

It would be a small miracle if the parents' feelings of estrangement were not in some way communicated to their children. Some elements of today's youth culture show signs of increased tension and alienation and decreased concern for property and human life. But the origins of these problems are much broader than parental feelings and puzzlement over changes in the Church. The approach taken in this book is to help parents identify and understand those factors which make an impact on children's development of moral values. Suggestions will be made as to how parents can work within the family context to promote a strong and responsible set of Christian values.

There are parents and youth who seem to have taken all these religious, educational and societal changes in stride. The children seem relatively respectful and stable, keep out of trouble and progress nicely in school. What makes for the difference? Sometimes there are no easily identifiable clues. Children grow differently, even within the same family. Some get into more mischief and seem to have to learn the hard way. Others have smooth sailings. So if parents have discipline problems with their children, this does not automatically mean that the parents are at fault. Too often, the parents who have tried the hardest are heard to ask sincerely, "Where did we go wrong?" And often enough, it is not those parents who should be so self-critical.

The purpose of this book is to provide parents with tools for better understanding their children and for nurturing the process of moral development. Many factors influence this process. The approach here taken will be to utilize research to identify these factors and then describe patterns which arise due to their influence during four periods of childhood. The findings of contemporary researchers in the areas of personal and moral development will be used to help parents better understand how to share their values with their children. It is essential that we seek to assist and support each other in this effort, if we are to be committed to the goal of developing a Church peopled by individuals who consciously make and take responsibility for their moral choices in accord with the teaching of Jesus Christ. To this end, this book is intended.

CHAPTER ONE: Fostering Moral Development in Today's Family

A recent national survey of over two thousand individuals of all ages and from over twelve hundred families documents some of the challenges facing today's parents. *The American Family Report, 1976-77, Raising Children in a Changing Society,* indicates that two of every three parents have problems communicating with their children in the crucial areas of drugs, drinking, sex, crime, death, family problems, and money. More than one in three parents say they are unsure of the way they are raising their children. Almost four in ten parents feel their children are less happy than they were when they were children.

The same study documents the different sets of values which seem to prevail in two types of American families, called the "traditional" and the "new breed." The traditionalist parents hold a slight numerical edge over the new breed parents. They tend to be stricter disciplinarians and are more child centered than the new breed. They value marriage as an institution, are willing to sacrifice for their children, and respect authority, religion, hard work and success. The new breed parents, however, profess to be more self-oriented, place less emphasis on marriage as an institution, and are less concerned with religion, patriotism and success. They are more permissive and tend to believe that children should be free to make their own decisions.

Both groups of parents however do agree that children should be taught the following values: duty comes before pleasure, authority figures know best, hard work pays off, sex outside marriage is wrong, and patriotism is right. This research is important in that it gives a thumbnail sketch of real differences in approaches to parenting. However, the conclusion of the study, that these contrasting groups of parents "are teaching their children the same set of traditional values," needs to be challenged.

The differences in what these two groups value are rather profound. Further, one must distinguish between the values these parents say they are teaching their children and the actual values the children develop. To determine what the children in fact do value would require a different research design based on their actions and on an in-depth analysis of how they came to their decisions. It is also important to recognize the changes which have occurred in certain structures, such as the family and the schools, for these changes do impact on how the child develops or fails to develop a responsible set of

Christian values.

The primary recommendation this book offers parents is that the most effective way to share Christian values with children is to provide them with the ability to weigh in the balance the various value tensions in society. This means that the parents need to train children to see the different values at work in the changes in society. Then the children need to develop the ability to recognize the similarity in what may appear to be opposite values. The hope is that the children will eventually see the strengths and weaknesses of each of the "opposites."

Parents can best share their religious values with their children by training them to see the values behind the different ways of approaching various actions. Too often, these opposites are neglected by a one-sided approach to Christian values. The traditionalist approach is deified and the new-breed approach is villainized, or vice versa. The approach suggested here urges that the tensions be put in the balance and that there be a dialectic or debate between the opposed values. In this chapter we will explain this approach by considering three basic tensions parents and children experience daily. Chapter two will then apply this same balancing or dialectical method to an understanding of Jesus' teaching on values and then to a psychological overview of how the individual develops values. Chapters three through six will then offer specific insights for understanding four age levels of children. Each of these chapters recommends specific practices for sharing values with children. The concluding chapter will summarize the balancing action which remains the constant source for development throughout the process of becoming Christian.

A. The Tension between Community Sense and Individualism

Family research expert Urie Bronfenbrenner has provided considerable evidence to document the fragmentation of the American family. This research is consistent with the findings of the above-cited study which evidenced that nearly two of every three parents surveyed believed adults should have lives of their own even if this necessitated parents spending less time with their children. Although this is clearly typical of the new breed parents, it seems also to be given credence by some traditionalists who typically identify themselves as child centered.

The increase in the divorce rate in American society is consistent with the philosophy of two out of every three parents surveyed who no longer believed in staying together just for the sake of the children. Such findings can lead one to suspect that what is at the basis of these changes in the approach to family is a simple matter of hedonistic selfishness versus responsible generosity. Clearly, respect for the individual has been fostered in the last two decades by popular psychologizing of self-actualization and existentialism. But to describe what is happening in today's society as egocentricity versus altruism, selfishness versus selflessness, is not only inaccurate but destructive. Before making a negative or condemnatory judgment about the meaning behind the above-quoted statistics and the two types of parents, consider the following.

Every family member really has two responsibilities: to self and to family. The two are not inconsistent but it is evident that there is tension between them. For example, the parent who holds a professional job may feel drawn to spend additional time on the job and this may well be at the expense of the children's needs. Similarly the adolescent may feel called to pursue personal needs at the expense of family togetherness. The challenge is for parents and, to the extent possible, for youths to balance these seemingly conflicting tensions. One approach which would help parents and children handle this tension is that of enlightened self-interest. In other words, the parent needs to understand his or her professional life in such a context as to realistically believe that authentic self-development comes through becoming a full person, not simply a professional person. This requires the parent to have a self-respect which comes from within and does not depend on or come from the job. This may seem unrealistic especially when the family's finances depend on the parent's professional success. Even in the face of such financial need, the parent's identity needs a basis other than that of breadwinner.

As for the adolescent, he or she needs an identity apart from the peer group and independent of family. The parents need to help the child experience what family historian Edward Shorter describes as the state of mind of the supportive family. In *The Making of The Modern Family,* Shorter distinguishes the nuclear family—mother, father, children—from other patterns of family life in Western society. The members of the authentic nuclear family share a special sense of solidarity that identifies that family as separate from the surrounding community. The members feel that they have much

13

more in common with one another than with any-one outside the family. By means of this sense of privacy they feel they enjoy a privileged emotional climate they must protect from outside intrusion.

The accent here should be on the privileged emotional climate in which the family members respect and want what is best for one another. If one overemphasizes protection from outside intrusion, a major problem develops. The problem with such an overly defensive approach to family is that it tends to become isolationist and creates a system which heightens the importance of family by denigrating outsiders. Typically this exaggerated approach fails to achieve its goal. Once the children discover they *can* share deeply with outsiders, they will conclude that they must separate themselves from the family and its isolation if they are to be true to their own values and to their newly discovered "brothers" and "sisters."

That balance and integration are here needed is evident in the second great commandment given by Jesus: Love your neighbor *as* yourself. The challenge here is to understand that the best way to further self-interest is to further the interests of family members and neighbors. This ideal, so reminiscent of the gospel call to "die to self" may seem unrealistic in light of the demands of the real world. But it's an ideal which calls today's parents and children to balance two values, the need for personal integrity or individuality and the need for a strong appreciation of the community, be it family or a broader group of persons such as neighbors or church community.

B. The Tension in Education between Content and Process

One of the major complaints voiced by today's parents in adult religious education discussions is that their children are not like they were when they were kids. An often-cited example of these differences is found in attitudes toward school. When the parents were young, children respected the authority of the teacher. If needed, the paddle was available to reinforce that respect. Parents often say, "They don't seem to learn anything in school." Of course, sometimes, this complaint is legitimate. But there is a deeper set of tensions below the surface of turmoil in the school, a set which makes an important impact on the youth's development of moral responsibility. That tension exists between the process of learning and the content learned, that is, between the *method* of asking and answering questions and the *content* of the answers expected.

When the Soviet Union launched its first satellite into space in 1957, American educators reevaluated their theory and practice. Until that time, rote-memory prevailed in teaching foreign languages and religion. Cookbook approaches were commonly used for teaching the sciences. Today, the conclusion of our best theorists and practitioners is that children learn better when the lessons begin with experiences and move toward conclusions. The traditional method had been just the reverse starting with a known fact and demonstrating its truthfulness. In a word, the deductive approach was replaced in many schools by the more experiential inductive approach.

15

Twenty years later one can see some school systems coming to the conclusion that their students seem no better off with the experiential method than with the traditional. The problem here is not a failure of the experiential approach as such but of its proper implementation. Oftentimes, the difficulty is that the students and teachers do not complete their homework. The experiential method is just as concerned with the content as was the traditional method, even more concerned. The difference is in the starting point of each lesson. The experiential method, whether in teaching science, language, or religion, can initially appear devoid of content; but if properly guided, the student will end up not only knowing the answers but also better equipped than the traditionalist student. The experientially trained student will know how to generate questions and will have a *method* for answering those new questions which will arise after leaving school.

Specifically, how do the principles of the experiential approach to teaching religion impact on the development of Christian values and moral responsibility? The scriptures of the Old and New Testaments, as well as contemporary Christian writers, stress that religious values must stem from the mind and heart and actions, from the total person. External behavior, such as the Old Testament sacrifices can of themselves be mere lip-service unless the motivation and understanding is authentic. In the words of St. Thomas More, the greatest tragedy is to do the right thing for the wrong reason. That was the lesson Jesus was trying to teach the Pharisees.

Practically speaking, in order to develop and engage the full person, the experiential approach

would not *start* by teaching the children to memorize the ten commandments. Rather, the first message would be that God is a loving Father who wants us to return his love and share it with neighbors. The children will still need to know each commandment and its meaning, but the meaning cannot be equated with the memory of the ten statements themselves. Authentic understanding requires that the person be able to generate the commandments from within. The experiential method asks this deeper commitment.

An important qualification must be made lest the principle of starting with experience be taken to an illogical extreme. If parents thought all knowledge must come through experience, the children probably would not live beyond their second year. Rules are needed. The toddler must learn that fingers on the range or in the electrical socket will be burned. Little children cannot understand the rationale behind some very important rules. To that extent it is necessary to adapt the experiential principle. A firm and traditional "No" may be the best starting point or experience for the child.

With that qualification in mind reconsider the impact of the school's emphasis on experience in the child's moral development. What would happen if a child were getting an experiential approach to many subjects in school, but the traditional dogmatic approach to religion? Two results are typical. The younger child will tend to keep out of trouble because of the motivation that should he do wrong the "God of the ambush" might strike him. However, when that child gets into the late teen years, and sometimes even as early as thirteen, he develops the mental ability to think logically and consequently tends to identify the fear-filled approach to morality as childish. This rejection of the authoritarian approach is a major reason why the dropout rate from church attendance is so high among adolescents. The authoritarian approach forced an either/or confrontation rather than a dialogue. The fact that the experiential method is still somewhat prevalent in today's schools puts pressure on teachers of religion to temper a strict "law and order" approach with a more democratic approach geared toward eventual self-determination.

A bit of hindsight is helpful here. The weaknesses in the traditional approach to teaching religion, forcing youth to comply with religious obligations, has been only too painfully clear to teachers on the campuses of religious colleges. Typically, the youth rebelled so violently against the authoritarian approach to religion that one could never find them, neither in a church nor at campus worship. Once away from the strong arm of conformity, they exercised their independence and tried to discover their own personal God. Often it took the full four years of college to reopen their minds to the possibility that religion could be beneficial and that there was a better approach to religion than what they had known as children. The traditional approach, with its enforcement of respect for institutions of whatever kind, initially seemed to bear fruit. Problems did not appear to exist. The youth conformed. The children were told: "Be seen and not heard," "Do what you are told." Too often the fruits of that message become evident during later adolescence in the youths' absence from all church-related activities.

Again and again, the theme must be resounded: balance is needed. Laws are not the opposite of experiences. Rather laws are best learned through experiences. This principle applies to all ages of youth, but with very young children, because of their limitations, aspects of an authoritarian approach sometimes must be implemented. The tension between these two approaches is beneficial if understood by parents who initiate experiences for their children so a similar understanding develops in them.

C. The Basic Tension: Authoritarian versus Non-authoritarian

We have considered two sets of tensions: individualism versus communitarianism and content versus process. Although each element can be complementary to the other, it seems they often are found opposed to one another in the family and school settings. Each of these elements: individuality, community, method, and process is a value. But there is a deeper pattern at work behind the human tendency to oppose values. It is a type of thinking in which the human mind tries to identify a value by contrasting it with another value. The history of Christian approaches to moral values is replete with examples of exaggerated contrasts between values which of themselves are not opposites. Some members of the early Church for example initially saw a conflict between Jews and Greeks, humanity and divinity, Law and Gospel. This is not to deny the very real differences and values which lie behind each of these words. But the point is that a balance or synthesis can be achieved without denying the unique value behind these elements. The contemporary Church and Christian parents face the challenge of affirming moral values without rejecting possible complementary values: to balance both freedom and responsibility, subjectivity and objectivity, principles and situations, traditional understandings and contemporary findings, and to then communicate this balance to youth.

For parents to be more effective guides in their children's moral development they should, whenever possible, avoid being strictly authoritarian. Much of the parental confusion described in the

American Family Report stems from the authoritarian personality. Authoritarianism is one of the major reasons a person will mistakenly oppose values which in themselves are complementary. Three characteristics of the authoritarian approach to morality are as follows: 1. to isolate what should be considered together; 2. to excessively depend on authority either by making oneself a bit of a dictator or by absolutizing another person or set of laws; 3. to live in one or two time-frameworks, the past, present, or future, but without integrating all three. It is this tendency in parents to isolate a part rather than deal with the whole picture, that teaches children how to become authoritarians. Each of the three characteristics is a form of isolation. The task of fostering moral development is one of helping children develop the ability to integrate old values with new experiences and new values with old experiences.

Because the children are growing, their mental and emotional capabilities are also expanding. Before getting to the specifics of what parents can do with children of various ages, the meaning of "Personal Moral Development" needs to be given special attention.

With an understanding of morality today, parents can then apply the contemporary research findings on child development to their own task of nurturing and fostering their child's moral development.

CHAPTER TWO: The Meaning of Personal Moral Development

Persons begin life incapable of making a moral decision. Their growth toward moral maturity is quite gradual. Experience indicates that children within the same family, generally receiving the same type of treatment from parents, none the less do turn out differently. This often surprises parents although a moment's reflection on the biblical stories of Cain and Abel, Jacob and Essau, and the Prodigal Son and his Brother suggests that these personal differences have always perplexed parents.

The question is what type of experiences causes one person to develop a mature and responsible set of values while a brother or sister develops a contrary set of values. This, indeed, is the problem and mystery of free will. No matter how well parents condition the home and social environment, the growing child can always rebel and develop a per-

sonal counterculture. From the introductory chapter it should be clear that one of the best ways for
parents to avoid this problem is to take a directive
but modified democratic approach to child rearing.
At least then, the child will not have the additional
pressure of finding an identity and set of values in
spite of or in order to spite the parents.

But what specifically does this nonauthoritarian approach to moral development mean? What
does it look like? What do child-rearing practices
have to do with moral development and values? As
suggested above, what this democratic approach
needs to look like varies with the child's age. Chapters three through six will describe it in some detail
for each age level considered. But first we must work
out what morality means today; then the following
chapters, dealing with child-rearing, can be properly understood and applied to the child's moral development.

During the last decade or so, the term, the new
morality, has been often bandied about. In one
sense, the new morality is a rediscovery of the biblical morality taught by Jesus. In that sense it is not
new at all. But there have been several shifts in emphases. The most basic seems to be an attempt to
correct a former imbalance. This bears some explanation.

Morality, as understood from biblical times to
the present, has always been concerned with how a
person attempts to respond to the needs of other individuals and of the community. One way of expressing this is to say that there are two aspects of
each moral decision, responsibility to the values of
the individual and to the values of the community.

Sometimes these elements of a moral decision are called "subjective," meaning personal, and "objective," meaning the laws of the community. In less helpful popularized terms, these two emphases have also been called the requirements of the particular situation and the general values or principles behind the requirements. The gospel story of Jesus walking through the grain field on the Sabbath illustrates these two tensions. The Jewish rule specified that absolutely no work could be performed on the Sabbath including picking grain. No matter what the needs of persons might be, the religious law, then thought to be the same as God's law, clearly forbad such behavior. The situation clearly identifies the two aspects of morality, person and law. Jesus's statement to the Pharisees who confronted him on the spot clarified the relationship of these two elements. He told them the law was made for the person, not the person for the law. These two principles, respect for persons and for laws, should not be seen as in opposition to each other. But when the authoritarian mentality absolutizes one of the two aspects, then the imbalance needs to be corrected. It would have helped the Pharisees in that biblical story, if they had recognized that the laws came from the sincere attempt of religious leaders to help others know God's will. By recognizing the human origin of the laws, the Pharisees would have been less absolute or authoritarian and more open to Jesus' corrective of the imbalance.

This biblical narrative is typical of many stories of how Jesus attempted to maintain a balance and proper perspective between the needs of the person and the community's laws. Both need protection: the hopes of the individual and the hopes of

25

the collection of individuals as expressed in the community's laws. In other stories, Jesus urged individuals to follow the law. He directed the healed lepers to wash and show themselves to the priests according to the law. So in contemporary moral theology, as in biblical times, there is an attempt to balance the two aspects and to avoid absolutizing one or the other.

In order to gain a firm understanding of what is meant by contemporary morality it is necessary to grasp the wider context, namely, what is happening in contemporary theology in general. For what is happening in moral theology is indicative of the more pervasive changes within the Church's understanding of its religious values. Some have described this corrective emphasis as a personalist approach, meaning the rediscovery of the first aspect of moral decisions, the subject or person, in contrast to the objective needs of the particular setting.

This personalism has been nurtured by advances in contemporary psychology, which are very much in line with the thrust of Jesus' teaching that laws are made for the person. So in one sense, the psychological understandings to be discussed in later chapters can be seen as a further unpacking of what this personal dimension of morality means.

When persons first hear this personalist emphasis, a common fear often raised is: "But isn't that subjective!" Subjectivism, however, is not the same as personalism. Subjectivism is when the person pays attention only to his or her whims and disregards the needs of the community and its laws. Subjectivism is a form of authoritarianism in which the individual proclaims self as the sole source of truth.

A great danger in subjectivism is that the individual often concludes that salvation is earned because of his or her good acts and personal moral life. This is quite contrary to Jesus' teaching about salvation and his Father. What was stunning about Jesus' words was that he addressed the Father as Abba, literally meaning Daddy, a term of intimacy nowhere used in the Old Testament. And second, Jesus showed us his loving Father as giving mankind salvation as a gift. It was free and not something we could earn by doing good works.

During the last decade national surveys of several Christian denominations indicated that most Christian adults did not believe this teaching of Jesus. Most seemed to believe that if a person gets to heaven, it will be because they deserve heaven as a reward for the good deeds they have performed. Once again, this points up the distinction between the personal and the objective or legalistic. Jesus announced that salvation was a gift, from the person of the Father to each human person. But many of today's adults feel more secure if they rely on their own objective good deeds. They feel more in control of their own destiny, more in the driver's seat, more authoritarian. Part of what is meant by saying contemporary morality is a rediscovery of Jesus' teaching is that it is based more on the personal generosity of the Father than on man's adherence to the laws, good and necessary as that adherence is.

What are some of the further implications of personalism for understanding morality today? There has been a shift in both understanding and language, from talking about sins to talking about sin. Moralists today still affirm the reality that per-

27

sons do commit sins. Evil is still rampant in the world and needs to be fought against as much now as ever. What has been better understood however is the source of evil in the heart of man.

At first consideration, this may seem quite traditional, and it is. But there is a subtle clarification contained in the shift, consisting in the recognition that the heart of man, including the person's intentions, is an important aspect of morality, along with the action itself. Intentions are not of themselves sufficient criteria or norms. Suppose for example that Adolf Hitler had good intentions. That would not have lessened the objective destruction he brought about. On the other hand, the action itself can not be judged in isolation from the intention. The problem here is simply that external actions of themselves do not tell somebody the meaning behind those actions. A person can participate in a liturgy because of a desire for "looking good." The objectively good act is subjectively corrupted by the bad intention. This distinction seems to have been what Jesus had in mind when he taught, concerning the issue of dietary laws, that it is what comes out of a person, namely out of the heart, that corrupts someone, not what goes into a person. Christ's concern was with the source of the morality, the person's basic disposition. Was it ego centered or other centered? Was it selfish or altruistic, greedy or giving? The individual sins which a person commits gain a large measure of their importance from the overall pattern of the person's heart or conscience. This rediscovered morality certainly calls each individual to strive to avoid all sins. But it also says we should not stop there but rather probe further and see if a deeper motivation such as pride or self-aggrandisement is not corrupting the person's spirituality from within.

The above consideration of the person-centered thrust of contemporary moral theology provides a necessary backdrop for this discussion of how today's parents can better enable their children to develop moral values. Now it is important to consider a similar shift, from talking about children "learning" values, to their "developing" values.

Is Value Developed or Learned?

Everyday speech uses phrases which describe parents who "teach values" and children who "learn values." But few of today's professional educators or trained religious educators would accept this way of speaking about values. They would prefer to speak of values as developed rather than as learned. The difference points to another important emphasis which once again implies a rediscovery of the person in morality. The difference stems from the understanding of values as originating primarily from inside the person rather than from outside. This distinction is very much at the heart of clarifying how parents can help their children become good Christians. Those who follow the learning approach to values tend to stress good example and to exhort youth to good deeds. This is well and good, but it is inadequate because authentic values cannot be learned. Parents who follow this approach often become confused and wonder what happened when their children grow up and seem to make all the wrong choices. They have understood value as a concrete habit, such as kindness which is readily identifiable through the good deeds that the person does such as helping family members, neighbors and others. The kind person would be seen as one who does the corporal works of mercy. Again, that of course is well and good. But, remember, such external behavior could be motivated by pride and egoism. Therefore, the authenticity of an act of kindness, because it stems from the recesses of the person's heart, can not be seen. And so it can not be simply modelled to another. That a child responds to parental pressure and does kind acts, does not necessarily mean the child has developed kindness. It must be developed from within after being encouraged by the example of family members and friends.

An additional problem is that when the children are young, such a learning-by-example approach to values is invaluable. Until the age of about nine years, the child tends to be relatively obedient, trusting and believing in most of what authority figures say. But from about the twelfth year forward, children are typically more questioning as they begin to differentiate themselves more and more from the family and to attach themselves to the peer group. This is when the child needs more than ever to be able to stand on his or her own two feet and to make decisions from within rather than by depending on the crowd or the parents.

The problem takes on an additional complexity because of the fact that the child changes as physical and social growth takes place. During the early years, until approximately ten, the child must to some extent be dependent on parents and authority figures to help and guide him or her in making decisions. But if the child has not been developing an internal guidance system, then that child probably has become overdependent on authority figures to tell him what to do. So what appears on the surface to be an obedient child can prove to be a conforming child who has not developed a strong conscience.

The answer to this issue is not for parents to choose development over learning. Both are needed. For the first ten years there needs to be an emphasis on both learning and developing. The child will be conforming more than making his or her own decisions. Then as the adolescent moves toward the late teens, what will emerge is the young man or woman who indeed is somewhat capable of making decisions based on an informed mind and a heart relatively free from the pressures of the peer group and a materialistic culture.

Before considering each of the age groups and how youth's values and morality develop during these stages, it is necessary to take a brief but closer look at what a value is. In one very general sense, a value is something for which a person lives or dies. Love of God, love of money, love of power could be examples of this type of all pervasive value. A value can also be described from the point of view of the processes going on when the person values. There are three actions the valuing person performs: seeing, cherishing and acting. By seeing is meant that the person clearly has and understands options. This means that the child or young adult who knows only one approach to religion or one way of acting does not really "see" because he doesn't know any better. The person who lacks options is like a prisoner. Free will is possible only when the individual can choose an alternative to what is at hand. Seeing clearly means that the individual is free from the internal compulsiveness which prohibits a person's ability to give the various choices due consideration. Valuing takes thoughtful consideration. Any forces which prevent this, whether they be from the inside or the outside, in the form of pressures of peers, family, or culture, all can detract from the individual's ability to make a free value choice.

The second action the valuing person performs is cherishing. This is where the person's ability to make decisions is central to becoming a person capable of valuing. But the kind of decision spoken of here is one motivated by the strong desire which comes from within the person rather than from an outside force. So valuing happens when the person really wants to do something despite the personal cost it may require. Or, it could be when the person simply thoroughly enjoys the action. The point is that the person who values really wants to do the act and is not simply confirming to outside or inside pressures.

The final activity that is integral to persons who value something is that they put their actions where their mind and heart are. They put their values into words and deeds and they do so repeatedly. The person who believes in a principle but is afraid to say so in front of friends values that principle less than one who is willing to speak up for it. Likewise, the person who will both speak up and then follow through in deeds is more deeply committed still. And finally, the person who is willing to exercise that commitment consistently over a period of time shows self to be more deeply committed than the person who does it only once and then forgets about it. For example, in some schools and churches, the poor are remembered in a special way at Thanksgiving time. This is excellent. But if it only happens once a year then it seems the poor are not very deeply valued by those Christians.

This last approach to values can be summarized as follows: values are beliefs that a person fully understands and freely responds to, not only intellectually, but also affectively and in actions. The valuing person sees, cherishes, and acts. A lessening of any of these aspects lessens the extent to which that person is truly valuing.

Each of the three considerations discussed in this chapter are important for understanding how parents can help their children develop their own set of Christian values. In summary, our goal is to enable youth to be personally responsive to the needs of others, to the community, and also to their own needs. But in order to do this, they need to be trained in how to see, cherish, and put their values into deeds. These skills in turn require development, not simply conformity. With these principles set forth, we can now consider each of four age levels.

CHAPTER THREE: Considerations for Parents of Preschoolers

In chapter one, we pursued the question of how parents can help their children develop religious values by considering two basically different types of families. Research identified a profile of the values each family said they held. We then considered one of the most fundamental differences in how these families raised children, the authoritarian as distinct from nonauthoritarian approaches. The conclusion was presented that the nonauthoritarian family tended to encourage children to be better able to make their own decisions, to stand behind them, and to be responsible to and respective of the community's values.

In chapter two, we examined three basic issues which provided a context for a discussion of how parents can foster moral values in youth. The first issue concerned the meaning of morality. It was explained that one theme emphasized in today's understanding of morality is the central importance of the meaning of person. Both the disciplines of theology and psychology have given us a clearer understanding and fuller description of what it means to be a complete human being, capable of identifying the needs of others and of taking responsibility for them.

The second issue which helped provide a context for this book's concern was the difference between developing values of one's own and learning conformity to another's values. Each was seen to have a place in the development of a person's character, although by itself, the learning approach to values and value formation was shown to be inadequate and even counterproductive as an approach to helping adolescents. The reason for that, and here we came to the third issue, is that a person's values are based on beliefs the person freely chooses. This view understands values as stemming from the person's thinking and cherishing and how both get translated consistently into words and deeds.

Where a parent stands with regard to these three questions, the meaning of morality, its development, and the process of valuing, partially describes whether or not the parent is authoritarian or nonauthoritarian. The more democratic parent takes the importance of the person into consideration when discussing family discipline and decisions. The nonauthoritarian parent wants the child to develop his or her own values rather than simply conform to parental values. And finally, the democratic parent presents the child with options for making decisions and shows appreciation for consistency between word and deed.

Given the establishment of this general context for valuing, what remains is the discussion of the specifics of how parents can foster religious values within their children. The difficulty of this task should be evident. For almost two thousand years, Christianity has followed a generally authoritarian approach to teaching morality: "Do good and avoid evil, or hell-fire will be your eternal reward." That approach did keep many potentially destructive actions from being committed. However, the conformity it demanded was the tip of the authoritarian iceberg which also kept many persons from becoming mature and morally responsible adults. The very fact that the "how" question is being asked today implies considerable dissatisfaction with the traditional fire-and-brimstone approach.

A second symbol of the difficulty in raising moral youth is evident in the recent establishment of three research centers designed specifically for the study of how youth develop values, the Boys Town Centers at The Catholic University of America, at Omaha, and at Stanford University. The Lutheran Youth Research Center in Minneapolis, as an example of other religiously sponsored programs, also attests to this same need. The official set of guidelines for Catholic religion teachers throughout the world, the *General Catechetical Directory*, indicates that the findings of research centers such as these should be incorporated into religion-teaching programs. The story of how religious values are best encouraged is not yet completed. But we have learned much that can be of help particularly in understanding how persons develop their intellectual and emotional capabilities. The assumption of this book is that the best foundation for being a religious person is to bring one's God-given capabilities to full fruition. Without that firm human foundation, the religious personality is like the house mentioned in the Bible which was built on sand.

What kinds of development are capable of happening in the preschool years? How can parents help foster that development? And how does that development support the growth of moral values? The importance of the preschool years was recognized and popularized by psychologist Sigmund Freud. He rendered our century considerable service by showing how many adult problems have their origins in difficulties experienced during the preschool years. This means that the preschool years are important for religious development because these years are the foundation for future development. What happens or fails to happen during these years can not be adequately compensated for in later years. Let's begin by exploring some specifics.

The infant begins by making choices, however rudimentary, practically from birth. Certain foods are preferred while others are rejected. Certain shapes and colors are attractive to the infant while others are ignored. High-pitched voices are usually preferred over low-pitched voices. By the sixth month, the infant has learned that it gets a good bit of attention from parents if it smiles and even more if it crys. So even at this early age, the child is building an attitude or disposition toward how to survive in this world. It is learning whether the world is full of wonder or is boring. It is learning patterns of social interaction such as whether others are going

37

to respond to its needs or are going to frustrate them. One way of describing the basic disposition the child gradually comes to by the end of the first year is that the child is either basically trusting or not trusting. A certain amount of each is necessary. But the scale should tip in favor of the disposition to trust.

Harvard University, in conjunction with several other universities, conducted a study of children's development that concluded that the first three years of life are the most important for the child's emotional and intellectual growth. These years need to be seen as the foundation for the child's later values. Should this finding be accurate, it will require a considerable shift in the educational priorities of church-related programs. To date, these early years have been the most neglected. Most religious personnel rarely come into contact with the preschool child until five years after the pouring of water at the christening.

The same Harvard research found that most parents although rarely trained in how to parent do a fine job during the infant's first eight months of life. It is almost as though nature protects the infant against many adverse influences within its environment, including parents' incompetencies. By the eighth month of life, practically every infant studied in the research had developed a powerful sense of curiosity. That is the age when the infant begins to crawl about the house and tries to get its hands on whatever it sees. Prior to this time, the study indicated, the parents' task is to take care of the infant's three most basic needs: 1. helping the infant to feel loved and cared for; 2. providing encouragement to learn specific physical skills; and 3. stimulating curiosity towards the outside world.

One key for the parents to keep in mind is that the infant's tool for gathering information and learning is its entire body. The infant learns if it is loved and supported through how it is picked up, held, patted, and generally physically engaged by family and other adults. The child's mental development during the first year consists of activities such as coordinating eyes with hands, judging distances, and crawling. During the first year, parents usually put few demands or restrictions on the child. We will see later how the child's resolution of the first year's conflicts impacts on the development of the adolescent's religious values. But first let's examine more closely what goes on in the first years and specifically what parents can do to help.

The way the parents can help the child to feel loved and cared for during the first eight months is by gently attending to the child's physical needs. The Harvard research concluded that practically no child is spoiled by the eighth month of life. This means that the eternal question of whether or not to let the squawling infant cry it out in the middle of the night, no matter how resolved by the parents, will not spoil the baby. On the positive side, what parents can do to encourage the child and at the same time make their own life much more pleasant is to celebrate the child's every day accomplishments. Specifically, when the child develops the ability to perform a new act the parents' supportive fuss speaks volumes to the child about its own accomplishments and esteem.

The following list, with approximate ages, will

give parents some idea of the type of accomplishments to expect and encourage in their infant's development. Every child is different, so the ages when the developmental task is accomplished may vary widely. The importance of this list is in outlining the accomplishments which parents should actively look for and encourage without pushing. This sensitive awareness can help both parents and infants live with a sense of celebration.

The thoughtful reader may raise the objection, "wouldn't all this positive support make the child tend to be overdependent on parental encouragement and support?" If the parents did nothing other than encourage the child to focus on its own accomplishments, then quite possibly the reader's objection would be justified. Parents who focus on nothing but support of the child can end up with a child whose self-esteem or ego is too large to fit into the family garage.

One way to temper or balance the celebration of accomplishments is to stress the need for control. The child, for example, must learn the meaning of "No." When the eight month old learns to crawl over to the dining-room table and to pull on the table cloth, celebration must give way to a firm "No." This can be done without inviting the newly mobile baby to feel condemned or rejected. The focus should be on the object, the tablecloth, not on the child.

The reader will recall that the three tasks of the parent during the first year were to help the infant feel loved, provide encouragement, and stimulate curiosity toward the outside world. The last of these, the outside world, is the corrective to overemphasis

Suggestions for Celebrations

Infant's newfound capability to:	Occurs
eat and nurse avidly............	in first week
smile socially	during second month
pause and watch while nursing	end of second month
reach and grasp for objects.......	in third month
repeat some sounds .... roll from back to side	in fourth month
accept small objects	in fifth month
play stick-out-tongue games......	in sixth month
recognize self in mirror .... reach, grasp, retrieve, and put object into mouth	in seventh month
reach, grasp, retrieve and play with object............. stack objects creep and crawl wave and say good-bye	between eighth and twelfth month

on the second duty, the providing of encouragement. The tablecloth is part of the outside world that is forbidden to the child's tugging. At about nine months the child will not understand that the glass that it has just broken by pulling it from the table is any less valuable than the unbroken glass. In fact, the broken glass may be more interesting to the child because of its sparkling in the sunlight. What is important is the stimulus and response behavior that the child will internalize. That cloth will begin to stand for something else, namely, the parental "No." And that "standing for" is a very important part of the sense of limits of the outside world which tells the child there is a difference between what it wants and what other people want. The importance of this experience of limits is crucial for later moral development.

During those early years there is no question that what traditional moral language refers to as sinning is not within the capability of the young child. The child has no concept of any objective value of things, persons or rules. Physical punishment does not significantly aid the child's comprehension but rather impresses the memory. During the child's second year, physical punishment should be used only as a last resort and only if a more serious type of damage or harm would result in its absence. If it is used, the parents should distinguish, as best they can, between the child and the deed. For example, the message parents give should not be that the child is naughty and therefore the object of the parents' disgust. Rather, it is the tugging on the table cloth that is naughty and to be rejected.

The parents' task, during all the preschool years, requires a continual balancing of these three challenges: caring, encouraging, and stimulating involvement with the outside world.

But there is a fourth general guideline parents can identify and use in developing their child's foundation for moral growth. That norm describes the close relationship which exists between the ability to use language and the ability to get along with people. Clearly, language of itself is not absolutely necessary because deaf persons and those with modest verbal capabilities can still get along. But it also seems to be clear that much of social interaction does depend on the ability to communicate with others, to listen closely to what they are saying, and to adequately express one's own point of view. At least some of the adolescent's and adult's moral problems stem from the frustration of not being able to adequately express one's point of view. The child who can not express anger verbally will tend to raise the fist in frustration. The adolescent who can not express love in words will tend to rely on more physical forms of expression. This inability is compounded by the fact that overdependence on the physical can become a habit or compulsion. Language gives a person the ability to gain distance on a problem, to elaborate possible causes and solutions to the problem. By reverting to the physical for quick but temporary relief, the youngster or adult can come to associate frustration with such forms of instant relief as indulging in sexual pleasures, alcohol or other drugs, or overeating.

So when the child of 18 months begins to push a block of wood around the kitchen floor and make kitty-cat sounds, it is the beginning of an important skill, the ability to let one thing represent another. It is the beginning of an imaginative form of language in which are found the seeds of successful social communication. It is the beginning of the use of imagination which will later generate the options needed for value decisions to be authentic as described in chapter two.

Toward the end of the preschool years, from ages three to five, parents often comment on the child's slowness to share playthings. Parents are

43

often dismayed by the selfishness of the child as evidenced in an unwillingness to share toys. Child psychologists sometimes call this aspect of childhood "narcissism without a Narcissus." By this they mean that the child, even the one year old, is self-centered but does not yet have a well-developed self-image. The child is selfish without actually having a self. The primary motivating factor of the preschooler is to strive for rewards and to avoid punishments. The concept of sharing seems quite beyond the child despite the fact that the child will occasionally use the word share accurately in speech.

When the preschool child does not share toys, authoritarian parents often use physical punishment. The initial result is that the child does seem to share the toys. The parents may be tempted to believe that they have met with some success. The problem here is that fear of punishment does improve memory and learning but not the child's development. The long-term effect of the punishment could amount to a conforming child but not one who has developed personal values. The short-term effect is that the parents have missed an opportunity to encourage the child to cooperate with others and learn the need for such cooperation. Again, a common sense warning must be made. In certain situations, conformity may be the only avenue open to the parents and child. But the norm is to foster growth and understanding by challenging the child. The parents need to present the child with a slightly broader understanding than he or she presently has.

Preschoolers, especially three year olds, are still quite suggestable. Therefore, parents can easily distract the child by asking if there is another toy that is fun to play with? Parents should have such a substitute in mind should the child's search fail. This approach is an early introduction to the skill of searching for alternatives. Also, it is a practical application of the principle of authentic valuing as explained in chapter two: valuing requires the ability to see alternatives. Children do not master this skill at age three. But parents in using their imagination to successfully resolve such minor conflicts as how to share toys, greatly help the child's ultimate moral development. Such parental patience avoids the trap of emotional turmoil and instead teaches the child how to face problems and challenges with a mind and heart clear of confusion.

CHAPTER FOUR: Considerations for Parents of Nine Year Olds

Why write about the fourth-grade child rather than the first or sixth grader? Primarily because that year around nine or ten years of age is one of transition away from a child's self-centered view of life and toward a more altruistic or other-centered adult view of life. Also, the fourth grade is when morality is traditionally introduced as a formal topic in most religious education programs. And further, it is during this year that the child's concept of friend takes on new meanings. All three of these developments are closely interrelated to each other and that is why this transitional year is particularly worthy of closer consideration.

But first, let's look over our shoulder to see what has happened to the child since the last chapter left off with a close-up consideration of the preschooler. The preschooler was described as self-centered in that the child's reference point for identifying what is important is self-pleasure. This sense of selfish goes beyond the moralistic sense usually associated with that term. What has happened during the first three years of grade school is that the social world of the child has had a population explosion. Not only are the classmates now a part of the child's world, but in a more significant way, so also are all those characters in the children's television programs and comic strips. These super heroes, in one sense, are an outgrowth, an expression, and a projection of the strong emotions sometimes felt by the preschool child. The media heroes are friendly relatives of the all-powerful monsters which the younger child may have complained of, those nocturnal creatures which the child imagined were lurking in the closet at bedtime. In a phrase, the toddler's narcissism, which was without a Narcissus, eight years later now has a Narcissus. Magic prevails in the life of the six year old. With this gradual opening toward social horizons, both real and imagined, the child of the early grade school years borrows a sense of identity and mastery from those mythical giants of stage, television screen, and athletic field. The psychological dynamics of how the child of the early grade school years thinks, namely in terms of these mythical roles, gives parents important clues to how to help the child develop a strong moral sense and religious values.

During the earliest grade school years, boys and girls retain much of their charming, gullible naivete. Typically, they are relatively easily led by authority figures. The parents and teachers, for example, can still share in the olympic stature of the child's worship of heroes. The child seems to live in a mythic world. He is more interested in the physical aspects of objects and persons than in abstractions. Friends in the here and now, for example, are still more important than the idea of friendship. Secret passwords are very important because they give the child a sense of being included in a group and in the power of the group. The child does not yet think successfully by means of abstract logic but rather haltingly by intuitions, associations, and untested generalizations.

Parents can get a closer view of their child's form of thinking by probing how he or she comes to a conclusion or answers a question. Suppose the parents and their child saw a popular dramatic film about wars between citizens of different stars and galaxies. Let's suppose that the greatest power described in the film is that "force" which holds the universe together. This force is described as available to those sensitive persons who can tune into its presence and its gentle movements within themselves. But for the child of these early grades, the force is not seen as a gentle spirit inclining a person to wisdom and to feel what is right to do. Rather, the young child thinks he or she can get a handle on the force and wield its power by having control of a specific object such as a magical light-sabre. This is called intuitive and concrete thinking because the child concentrates on selected aspects of the film's story, namely, those which are written large and display power such as physical strength or athletic skill. The child passes over and leaves out those elements of the story which do not fit his own intuitive feel for power and for belonging on the side of the good guys. The young child then associates the force with the magical beam of light wielded by the

49

story's heroic characters. If the child were older, say thirteen, he would not so easily neglect other information given in the film which describes and defines the force. The nine-year-old child is closer to the mythic world than to the logical world, closer to outside heroes than to internal logical order, closer to what people, powers, and forces can do for him than what they are in themselves.

Consequently, the child's religion is still characterized by a readiness to experience the miraculous aspects of life. Part of the child's simplicity is that the miraculous aspects of many of the biblical stories remain unquestioned. The child associates the Bible's stories of God's dramatic and powerful interventions with divine power. The child believes that it happened exactly as the Bible tells it. For example, for the fourth-grade child, God did make the waters of the Red Sea separate and stand as two great walls while the Old Testament Israelites escaped from the Egyptian army. Further, the research of religious educator Ronald Goldman found that the nine year old typically imagines that God accomplished this feat by having his arms act as barriers holding back the waters. The physical, once again, is what the child is capable of concentrating on. The divine force, seen as very large and in sweeping gestures, is then imagined as withdrawing and the water as doing His will in crushing the Egyptian soldiers.

What should parents do in this situation? The position taken here is that parents should not encourage this literal approach to Scripture. Nor should they simply attempt to pull the rug from beneath the child's feet. This magical approach is what the child's development allows at this point. What parents should do is ask gentle probing questions which eventually will help the child move beyond such concrete forms of thinking. A parent could, for example, ask the child whether any of the Egyptian soldiers were good men. The typical answer would tend to be "No, they were all bad." Pharoah in particular is seen by the child as evil. The nine year old, thinking in concrete terms, literally identifies each person to be good or bad, perhaps for the sake of following the plot. Such literalism, which identifies good and evil all too simply, will eventually be outgrown. But for now, the fact that the Exodus story portrays God as "hardening Pharoah's heart" does not bother this youngster. But by the time the child is eleven, he or she quite typically will be wondering, "Was that fair?" That is when parents would stand in good stead to know a bit more about the meaning of the Old and New Testaments.

Another question parents can ask which illustrates the kind of question that can simmer in the nine-year-old's mind is, "Do you think any of the Egyptian soldiers were daddies?" Since for many young children, daddies are always good guys sharing in that mythic olympian power, it will be a little more difficult for the child to lump an entire group of people into second-class citizenry? Such categorizing into absolutes relies on stereotypes and seems to be a necessary phase of the child's development. What parents need to avoid however is unnecessarily prolonging this period of literal interpretation of biblical stories. They also need to help the child avoid generalizing about groups of people and to avoid teasing other children because of their physical characteristics.

What if parents are themselves convinced that everything in the bible did indeed happen in exactly the way it is told? Such convictions are here seen as detrimental both to the parents' and child's faith. Besides being contrary to the research findings of biblical scholars and common sense as well, a literal interpretation of every story of the Bible will probably eventually become an obstacle for the adolescent who learns to use logic in the service of his or her religious convictions. All too frequently, for example, the teenager stops taking the Bible as "gospel" and then totally rejects its wisdom as preposterous. The thinking youth then feels pressure to reject the literal-minded adults because they seem too naive. Research with adolescents indicates that it is in the two or three years after this tenth year, when logic is beginning to take greater form, that the early adolescent begins to move away from what he or she judges to be childish religion.

When the child is nine however, the biblical stories are still to be enjoyed as celebrating the joy of God's generosity toward mankind. Parents need to take some care lest the theme of the chosen race foster the youngster's already egocentric approach to life. The accent should be on celebrating the truth of God's power. Any other logic generally should be held in abeyance unless the child raises questions. The parents' first responsibility is to help the child come away from the stories, prayer service or liturgy with a strong conviction that God is powerful, does love each person individually, and does call each person to be his special friend. These convictions have their own beauty and truthfulness.

This discussion of how the child tends to think can benefit from further elaboration on what has happened to the child's moral sense during those first three years of grade school. During that time, the child has gained a second criteria for what it thinks is morally right or wrong. Initially, the pre-schooler has only one strong norm, which is outside self, namely whatever pleases or displeases the parents. But as the child develops a stronger sense of identity, however fragile and mythical that may be, the child is also gaining gradually the ability to please him or herself. By fourth grade, this sense of pleasing self, pleasing the young Narcissus, is rather well established. Pleasure becomes a norm for determining what is good. To this age child if going to church is not a pleasurable experience, if it is "no fun," then going to church is "no good."

This dependence on the physical is a clue to how parents can help their children develop a sense of religious values, namely through the physical setting. Suppose for example parents want the child to value prayer. Parents should accent the physical by the lighting of a candle, dimming the lights, and creating quiet. It all appeals to the child's sense of magic. What the child does not yet understand through logic, parents can make up for by means of atmosphere or physical setting. Religious values are developed by experiences, not by logic.

For example, one of the more difficult religious values for parents to share with children of this age is the ability to look at a problem or situation from another's viewpoint. If the nine year old feels he was wronged by a playmate, he may take an eye-for-an-eye stance against that other child, even if the original transgression was an accident. A parent often gets no response when asking the wronged child, "How would *you* feel if *you* accidently broke someone's toy and then that person tried to get even with *you?*" Instead the parent needs to encourage the child to talk with the offending playmate and to hear an "I didn't mean it" or an "I'm sorry" directly from the child.

A second obstacle to valuing which the nine year old must begin to dismantle is stereotyping. In one sense the child of nine has already learned that teachers, daddies and mommies do sometimes stray from their heroic patterns of living. They do make mistakes which the children will be quick to point out. Why then do the nine year olds continue to interpret some groups of people in such extremes of virtue and vice? Why is it that they tend to think that a minister, pope, president, star athlete, or rock singer can do no wrong? Such idolization continues because those categories of people are ideal and abstract. They are beyond the young child's concrete abilities. Further, because the child does not have a firm identity of its own, these dramatic *personae* are kept as models until the real self emerges during the later teen years.

The child's moral direction at this young age is set more by external example than by internal free choice. The child decides what is right or wrong primarily by how parents will react, how it pleases them, and also with a view to how it pleases the child's friends. The child has difficulty coordinating two norms simultaneously. If parents lay down a rule for family members, and then a few days later they make an exception to that rule, the child will be quick to protest what it sees as unfair. The child has trouble balancing the intention or purpose of the rule with how to apply that rule in a particular situation. Typically, the child of eight or nine judges the seriousness of an offense by the extent of the damage caused. For example, the child usually considers breaking three bottles accidentally to be worse than breaking one bottle intentionally. What can parents do about this? Telling the child that intentions are just as important as actions is usually beyond the child's comprehension. Unless the child has already developed a stronger self than most nine year olds, the importance of intentions does not have a firm enough foundation. So the child can not learn to be moral unless a stronger self has already developed.

The virtues which seem to be needed by parents of nine and ten year olds are consistency, patience, joy, and understanding. These skills can be utilized in celebrating, in putting the child to work, and in assigning those concrete and specific meaningful little jobs which give the child a sense of importance, belonging and identity. Through concrete gestures the child gets a full message which does not demand the ability to think abstractly. In this way, the parents are doing what they can to help foster a stronger self, to help the child feel at home in making value judgments with some degree of thoughtfulness and love, and in translating these values into deeds.

CHAPTER FIVE: Considerations for Parents of Junior High Children

The youngster between the ages of twelve and fourteen typically is attending the junior high school classes from seventh to ninth grades. This period, like the preschool years, contains a spectrum of children's behavior, thinking, and valuing. But there are common themes which can be described without assuming that they apply equally across that spectrum. There is, for example, a charm and frustration typical of this aged child that begs to be considered. The charm stems from the idealism and enthusiasm of early adolescence. The frustration stems from their inability to coordinate their ideals with their own behavior and with the needs of the situation in which they find themselves.

Physically, the youngster often feels somewhat self-conscious. The onset of puberty causes a number of physical developments which make them vulnerable to self-doubts and unfavorable comparisons within their peer group. Twelve-year-old girls, for example, typically slightly taller and more verbally skilled than their male counterparts, may cause boys to feel a bit of competitive pressure. All of these changes, the challenges of transition from childhood to the more adult-like teenage society, call for more coordination and sorting out than the youth can successfully muster.

At this age level the focus of moral development is on the thinking processes and feelings which are the seedbed of the youth's values. Recall that the ten-year-old child considered in chapter three was very dependent on stereotypes to help him or her organize thoughts and actions. This pre-logical and concrete style of thinking left the child without comprehension of the rational basis for rules and with a particular vulnerability to dependence on the dictates of the group. The basic struggle the twelve or thirteen year old faces is how to be self-reliant rather than dependent on the peer group. And yet, one of the junior high school youngster's greatest fears is to be rejected by the group. So it is to be expected that researchers of this age period find most of the children having a strong inclination toward conformity to the group. For the early adolescent, authentic values are still somewhat beyond reach. Their freedom to see clearly is limited as is the ability to see a project through to completion. This is normal for this age level and to be expected, although not encouraged.

What then can parents do about overdependence on the peer group? The most effective long-term contribution parents can make is for the parents themselves to have a strong and well-developed sense of their own identity. Psychologists who have worked with parents and children together, that is, who have counseled the family as a family, have found that certain emotional strengths and weaknesses are passed down from generation to generation. Emotions, which to a degree are really learned responses to situations, tend to be learned from parents. So parents who tend to be conformists usually have children who are conformists. Parents who have a strong self-identity usually have children with strong identities who can better withstand the peer pressure to conform. Even at the age of twelve, before a firm sense of individual identity dawns for most children, there will be individual differences in how these youth will be able to withstand pressure from peers.

At this point, three qualifications are in order relative to how parents can and can not influence their children's development of values.

1) Parents whose children seem to get into trouble should not conclude from the above that they, the parents, are to blame. In spite of the above suggestion that parents do to some extent influence the basic level of the strength of their children's independence, parents can not logically blame themselves for their children's shortcomings in this regard. If parents were to blame themselves, then they should be logical and continue to pass the guilt-buck back to the grandparents and beyond to earlier and earlier ancestors. The purpose here is not to establish guilt but to identify the source of the child's moral backbone within a parent-child con-

text and within a discussion of self-identity or the ability to stand against the crowd if need be.

2) Parents again need to distinguish between the behavior the youngster performs and how the youngster came to the decision to so act. The twelve year olds can seem to be identical in their moral behavior, they can both do the same thing such as joining an environmental clean-up operation. The first youngster however, may simply be conforming and joining the crowd. The second could be doing it on the basis of understanding and conviction. Parents can help youngsters by being sensitive themselves to which type of motivation is at work in jobs around the house. Parents can sensitize children to this distinction by asking questions which will help the children to see the motivational aspect of their involvement in such clean-up projects.

3) There is a third qualification which must flow from this idea that the parents extent of identity influences the stability and strength of the child's identity. Some parent-child clashes are inevitable regardless of what kind of identity strength the parents and children have. Children need to distinguish themselves from others, to get out from under the shadow of others, lest they feel themselves fading away. With the increased dependence on peers which is so typical of the junior high period, these early adolescents sometimes use their parents as sounding boards and assurances that they, the youth, are somehow their own persons. Sometimes they complain to peers about their parents' strictness such as early curfew, which simultaneously wins peer acceptance and breathing space from parental authority. Yet, if some night they

want to go home because of tiredness or uncomfortableness with the group, the parents serve as an out. So parents should not automatically assume that the testing or rebellion of the junior-high-age youth is a personal attack against them. Rather, a certain amount of it is inevitable and needs to be handled objectively and, most importantly, without allowing escalation.

With these three general qualifications being made, what other forms of behavior typify the junior high youth? For one, there is often a gap between their ideals and real behavior. Typically, these children exhibit enormous bursts of energy which may remind adults of the enthusiasm of a lynch mob in the oldtime cowboy films. For example, the youth proclaim that they, as an army of environmental messiahs, will redeem the landscape from pollution caused by insensitive adults. Teachers, who have considerable experience with this age level, say these youth have the unique ability to declare war against pollution in the morning and then thoughtlessly throw candy wrappers on the classroom floor in the afternoon. These are the same children who get caught up in the enthusiasm of talking about a class project such as helping out at a home for the elderly. But when the day comes for the actual visit to the home, their thoughts often have long since turned to other good intentions and ideas. Few remember the original class project.

These examples evidence a certain degree of lack of continuity and commitment as well as an irresponsibility which can frustrate parents. It seems as though the commonplace household chores, washing dishes, doing laundry, vacuuming rugs,

61

and washing the car appear too lackluster to hold the thirteen year old's interest. Closer examination of these examples points to several contributing factors which can help parents better understand and work with this age level.

There are three steps parents can take to help their junior high youngsters develop values. The first involves an awareness that logic is now possible but its application needs to be encouraged. The youngster, who wants to be environmentally minded and yet creates a trashy classroom or bedroom, clearly has not yet applied the definition of environment to the commonplace settings of school and home. Remember, this youngster thinks in concrete terms, not in abstractions. Therefore, he or she will have a tendency to utilize false categories such as environment considered strictly in terms of grassy meadows and babbling streams. Here again, the parents' assistance is needed to nudge the early adolescent. Parents can help them first to see the consequences of not cleaning up at home and in school. Second, parents can help adolescents to become dissatisfied with excluding home and school from their understanding of what is meant by the word environment. But in such parental assistance, whether in the form of guiding the youth to learn from their mistakes or in explaining the inconsistency of their ways, it is most important for parents to avoid putting the child down. If given adequate emotional support, early adolescents will eventually understand and will get the job done.

A second step parents can take to help their youngster develop values at this age is to combat the child's tendency to categorize too quickly. The mind that over-categorizes does so by isolating a part of the picture and excluding important elements. For example, a twelve-year-old girl was told to help her brother do the dishes. Her job was to stack the dinner dishes and remove the food from the table. Her brother, in turn, was to wash the dishes. She removed the food to the kitchen, stacked the plates and gathered the silverware, but then left them on the dining room table. She took the parents' command, "stack the dishes," literally and in isolation from the overall sense of the job that needed to be done. She protested vehemently that carrying the dishes into the kitchen was not her job.

Such an approach to a task, which defines too narrowly and isolates the part from the whole, is not in itself a moral problem or sinful. But it certainly is a moral problem in that it can be at the root of family disunity, hurt feelings, and lack of initiative in taking responsibility. One short-term solution to these types of problems is to spell out in detail the child's responsibility. The child will learn what she is to do in that particular situation but probably will not develop the sense of responsibility for the task at hand. A more productive short-term approach is to help the youngster overcome the tendency to isolate jobs by being shown the need, "the dishes need to be washed," and allowed the opportunity to work it out. The child will then discover how to share responsibility with whomever else is involved.

A third step parents of early adolescents can take to help them develop a strong sense of values is to personalize functions and institutions. Persons who tend to categorize, whether of junior high age or adults, usually also tend to functionalize. By this is meant, they forget that certain tasks or responsibilities are done by people who have lives, needs, and hopes of their own, apart from the particular job they are doing at a given moment.

The categorizer, for example, may see parents as nonpersons whose divinely appointed task is primarily somehow to provide for the youth and benevolently ride herd on them. Examples of youth's functionalization of adults would be their thinking that parents, teachers, religious and clergy do the things they do because that is their job. What the categorizer is missing is the spectrum of internal motivations these adults may have.

This leads to many problems. The store owner's needs, for example, are not easily recognized by this approach. They are not dramatic nor written large for the young mind which is so dependent on both. The youth probably has not yet thought through to the fact that shoplifting deprives the storeowner of a certain amount of money needed for mortgage, salaries, and stock purchases. So there's a tendency on the youth's part to be concerned only with his end of the stealing, namely, not getting caught. This is why it is crucial to let these children see the personal side of parents and institutionally related persons such as store owners and religious personnel. Therefore, if parents can encourage some friendly interaction between the youth and the adult persons behind the roles, then the youth's fidelity to those persons will have a firmer foundation in the personal meeting. At this age, role models are an important avenue for exposing youth to a diversity of values and for building a firm foundation for their own valuing.

For a moment, let's look at the negative side of this. What happens when the three avenues for moral development suggested above are not utilized? Usually, alienation begins to spread. To begin with, junior high youth often have a difficult time living with themselves. They sense that their personal identity has not yet jelled and they often feel an urge to "be somebody." The family's approach to religion needs to speak to this deep-felt need for acceptance in three ways.

First, the child needs to feel genuinely affectionately accepted by whatever group he is with, family, playmates, or classmates. Parents can not control their children's environment outside the home. But they can encourage the school teachers or parish religious education program directors to foster among the youth this sense of welcoming one another. Research completed at the Boys Town Center at the Catholic University of America surveyed youth of several religious denominations. The study, conducted by Dean Hoge and Gregory Petrillo, searched for patterns in why youth participated in or avoided church-related programs. The teenagers polled indicated that the most important factor in motivating them to participate in these programs was the warm reception they received from the other youth already involved. Follow-up talks with the program leaders indicated that the programs having the greatest percentage of participation had leaders who in fact encouraged a sense of fellowship among the youth. This acceptance of the youngster, not to be confused with accepting shortcomings, is crucial for keeping the youngster in close communication with the parents and open to the personal values of organized religion.

A second characteristic of the successful program, became evident in the follow-up talks with the leaders. Those programs which were activity oriented flourished, while the more passive classroom-oriented programs hardly held the students' attention. This finding is true to psychologist Erik Erikson's insight that "industry" is what helps the youth stave off inferiority and paves the way to their identity.

A second way that the family's approach to religion can speak to the child's need for acceptance is to emphasize the acceptability of diversity within the church. Because the youngster has a tendency to overdepend on categories and to interpret laws literally, he or she may think there is only one right way of praying, singing, or worshiping God. Hence a worship program with guitars and folk songs, can be absolutized by the youth. Parents can help by exposing the junior high youngster to different kinds of worship and liturgies and different kinds of clergy, religious and laity. The youth who sees his or her parents accepting such diversity within the Church will get the rather direct message that there is room for the young adolescent's approach as well.

A third message which can help the youngsters overcome alienation from self, family, and Church is to present them with an image of God as someone who loves them even more than they love themselves. The youngsters hunger to be told that they are important. The gospel stories of how Jesus treated everyone respectfully, whether sinner or saint, male or female, older or younger, certainly can deliver that message.

Throughout the child's development, there are certain periods or phases which seem particularly difficult for both the child and the parents. The second, fifth, and twelfth years, for example, stand out in many parents' minds as particularly trying. The term the "terrible two's" suggests the troubles and temper the toddler gets into while exploring where personal autonomy ends and parental authority begins. The five year old similarly has newfound wings which lift him or her to test the limits of the parents' authority over them. The twelve year old or sixth grader, of all eight primary grades, is the most likely to end up in the principals' office for discipline problems. This last form of acting out can mark the threshold of the junior high years. The youths' preference for extremes and exaggeration incline them to either love or hate other persons and institutions. Therefore, fairness and consistency is what parents will particularly need in helping these youth leave aside their dependency on categorization and exaggeration. And because they feel accepted by their parents, these junior high youth can confidently explore the meaning of life from a point of view other than that of their influential peers and so can begin to formulate their own system of values.

CHAPTER SIX: Considerations for Parents of Senior High Youth

When children reach the age of fifteen and enter later adolescence, the hopes and fears of parents are usually heightened. By late adolescence youth are quite mature physically, but experientially, mentally, and socially, they still have much more to learn. Because parents are well aware of the differences between physical and mental development, and because children are less sensitive to these differences, there are bound to be conflicts.

Over the last several decades there has been extensive research on adolescence conducted by psychologists, sociologists, and social psychologists. Their findings have traced a shift in the very meaning of adolescence, a shift of which parents need to be appraised if they are to avoid handling today's new questions with yesterday's outdated answers. One such shift has been in determining the processes that take place during adolescence. During the first half of this century, adolescence was accurately described as the time when the growing young man or woman began to question the traditional values of adult society. During the later teenage years, the adolescent left behind the self of childhood which typically gained parental approval by an unquestioning obedience to parental authority. The youth's inner voice of conscience gradually became clearer and stronger. Eventually, various forms of conflict between parent and child became evident. The conflict between the youth's inner voice of conscience and adult society's outer traditions became like hammer and anvil, between which the young adult's self was forged.

However, for the current generation of adolescents, that description no longer seems accurate. Researcher and theorist Edgar Friedenberg, in his classic work *The Vanishing Adolescent,* concluded that the adolescents of more recent decades are marching to a different beat. No longer do they seem to arrive at self-identity through rebellion against adult society. No longer can adolescence be described as beginning with the young person's conflict with adult society and as ending with the youth's achievement of a coherent and clear sense of personal values.

Today, the consensus among researchers of adolescence is that adolescents have established their own society, with its own ideals, styles, and values. Two cardinal "virtues" of this youth culture seem to be what researcher Charles Stewart in *Adolescent Religion* described as: playing it cool and not sticking one's neck out. Both virtues are passive and result in a youth culture which feels it does not need rebellion against adult society. Rather, these virtues and the total youth culture would seem to encourage youth's replacing one form of conformity with another. That is, early childhood's conformity to adult traditions is replaced by later adolescence's conformity to youth culture. If that in fact happens, the teenager will reach eighteen years of age without the ability to think critically and stand on his or her own values.

There is evidence that considerable numbers of youth have given in to conformity and overdependence on peers. A study of over fifteen hundred youth by Joseph Adelson concluded that American adolescents by and large, are ill prepared to do much individual thinking concerning values. The need this type of finding points to is one reason why the accent of this book has been consistently on what earlier was called a dialectic. Adults need to foster individuality by training young children to pay attention to differences and to see the values inherent in opposite viewpoints.

Let's take a closer look at what these youth profess as important values. Let's chart how these values change as the youth pass from early to late adolescence. Social psychologist Milton Rokeach tested the value rankings or prioritizing of over eight hundred youth. The two charts below indicate how the youth compare the relative importance of the values. The numbers represent the median scores or mid-point measures for how the youths ranked eighteen long-range and eighteen short-range values. The charts below show those values which change across the years of adolescence and which are particularly pertinent to our study of how youths' moral values develop. The meaning that each of these individual values has will vary somewhat from child to child, so this study by Rokeach is by no means flawless. But parents and religious educators can gain an overview of how youth claim the importance of certain values increases or decreases during adolescence.

The findings confirm the shifts many parents say they witness. The older youth say they pay less attention to being cheerful, helpful, obedient, loving, forgiving, honest, and family oriented. It is almost as though they consider these values too childish and so want some distance from them. Notice for Table One that each of these values ranked high when the youth were eleven years old and then decreased as the youth became older. The seventeen year old, Table Two indicates, gives higher priority than younger teens to these values: self-respect, ambition, broadmindedness, responsibility, independence, and a sense of accomplishment. The eleven year old is relatively unconcerned with these values, not yet having developed a sense of self-direction. If one steps back from the charts, one can see that the picture of the eleven year old is consistent with the classical developmental theory of child psychologist Erik Erikson. The eleven year old has not yet faced the identity crisis but instead borrows an identity by cheerfully identifying with authority figures. He is anxious to be a helper and is relatively unconcerned about self-identity as such. So long as the parents and teachers of this fifth-grade child give him signs of positive affection, he is happy.

Youth's Value Rankings

TABLE ONE
Values Which **Decrease** with Age

AGE:	11	13	15	17
cheerfulness	6.5*	9.8	11.2	11.1**
helpfulness	6.5	6.5	8.1	9.1
obedience	11.3	10.1	11.9	12.7
love	4.8	5.7	5.6	7.2
forgiveness	7.6	8.6	7.9	9.5
honesty	4.6	4.5	4.5	5.9
family orientation	5.2	3.5	5.3	7.5

*Roughly speaking, this means that for half of this age group, cheerfulness gets a rank of sixth place (among 18 values) or higher; for the other half, it ranks lower.

**By age 17, for half of the group, cheerfulness gets a rank of 11th or higher; the other half ranks it lower. Cheerfulness has thus slipped in overall importance to youth as they get older.

All these differences in rankings are statistically significant at the .01 or .005 levels.

TABLE TWO
Values Which **Increase** with Age

AGE:	11	13	15	17
self-respect	12.2	11.6	9.7	8.4
ambition	10.0	7.3	7.1	6.2
broadmindedness	11.7	13.2	11.6	8.4
responsibility	9.3	7.8	7.5	7.4
independence	10.5	11.8	9.8	8.8
accomplishment	13.2	11.5	11.8	9.4

All differences are significant at .01 or .001 levels.

Erikson characterizes the adolescent's growth toward maturity as a coming to terms with two sets of tensions. The first set is called industry versus inferiority. The eleven year old who is given responsibility for specific household, scholastic, or athletic assignments and who fulfills them successfully tips the balance in the proper direction toward industry. This child gains a sense of competence from doing "things" and thereby does not succumb to a sense of inferiority. Because of the concrete actions, he or she can say "I've done it."

The second pair of tensions is called identity versus identity-confusion. The fifteen-year-old adolescent begins asking questions such as "Who am I?" "To what persons, things, and beliefs am I committed?" In the Rokeach study of eight hundred youths, the older youths increasingly became concerned with self-respect. This reflects the continuing emergence of the "Narcissus," but now with considerably less egocentricity. Parents could take some comfort in the increased concern the fifteen and seventeen year olds seem to have for the value of responsibility. But, as parents and teachers know so well, these youths are the ones who insist on defining what is meant by responsibility. Their ranking of the value independence shows this increased striving for self-reliance. This is a mixed blessing and creates new waves in the parent/child exercise of authority. If the older adolescent has not yet matured socially and needs to gain in prudence, then he or she should not be given a totally free hand to do whatever seems appropriate. If left on his or her own, the norms this youth would come up with would be inadequate.

Recently an informal survey asked high school religion teachers and youth ministers to report some of the statements they hear which seem to be typical of the adolescents they work with. Admitting the fact that many adolescents do not agree with these statements, the following "moral guidelines" none the less do seem to be commonly accepted among adolescents: "It's all right as long as nobody gets hurt." "Everybody's doing it." "It's my body, I can do what I want." "I couldn't care less." Notice that the experience of these teachers confirms the researchers' findings and theory described earlier. Among some youth there is considerable reliance on the peer group for norms. Some of the quotes also indicate considerable passive resistance.

The contemporary research of developmental psychologists Jean Piaget and Lawrence Kohlberg has identified one source of this conformism to be in the literalisms and concrete thinking which is typical of children from the ages of seven to the later teens. This inability to handle abstractions, such as principles, turns the youngster's mind toward "conventional" moral norms found written large in the peer group's culture. A characteristic of this age and level of moral development is the inability to understand the principles of law and order. The teenager can recite the commandments and the laws of home and school but does not actually understand the full implications and consequences of following or breaking the laws. This is part of what is meant by the fact that the youth are still maturing.

There is however a new development reflected in the teachers' portrayal of contemporary adolescents which is also confirmed by contemporary research. The statement, "I could care less" is indicative of a development of considerable importance. It indicates contemporary youth culture's contention that it can get along by ignoring the moral values and dictates of society. This passive resistance is what researcher Edgar Friedenberg sees as a new element in contemporary adolescence.

Decades ago, when adult society was more authoritarian, when the word of teachers and parents was final, the adult's word could not be ignored. Authority was so widely respected that any reprimand a youth received at school was reinforced at home. Any misbehavior in public, whether in the neighborhood streets, at the corner grocery, or in the parish church would surely result in a phone call to the home from some irate adult. Adult society no longer presents a united front. This fact, along with young people's higher mobility and youth oriented "institutions" ranging from beaches to discos, encourages youth to bypass adult authority.

The core problem that is here being surfaced for consideration is as follows. Youth who pass through their teen years without having had to think through the meaning of Christian values, practices, and doctrines will arrive at physical adulthood without a Christian basis for spiritual maturity. Further, they will not have the benefit of having developed their own personal values because they will have learned and conformed to a set of hand-me-down values from their peers.

Conscientious parents whose youth seem to have fallen prey to this conformism would do well to recognize that reversing the pattern may take years, just as it took years for it to develop. Biblical stories and the lives of certain saints such as Saint Paul may suggest that prayer can tempt God to send a lightning bolt and knock a prideful offender off his high horse. But even with Saint Paul, his story of having been converted when knocked from his horse is only half the story. He was not truly converted at that time. Rather he subsequently went into seclusion for several years of prayer and meditation. Only after that lengthy retreat did he feel confident in his newfound values and so take up public preaching and writing. Prayer for conversion is necessary but it needs to be reinforced by other forms of assistance.

The discussion so far has concerned itself with only a segment of the youth culture. It has focused on those adolescents who strive for their identity without the benefit of open communication with their parents and without the support and guidance of Christian values and practices. The question remains for parents of such youth: What can be done to help these youth develop their values in line with the ideals of Christianity?

Parents can look to two sources of hope, two avenues through which divine assistance seems to operate, in such cases where an on-going conversion is needed. These two sources are the role models with whom the youth comes into contact, and the youth's receptive value system which seems most open to developing values when encountering a powerful person or persons and a certain type of powerful idea. These two sources in effect represent first a social and then a psychological means of change. Again, we turn to the work of Milton Rokeach who has researched both of these means for fostering change in an individual's value system.

77

Rokeach and others found that an effective way to help open a closed mind is to immerse the young person in an environment which supports him as a person regardless of his values. This allows the individual to lower his defenses. The youth is then attracted to the positive values, that are embodied in the personable adults who support him.

The second source of hope is to be found in exposing the young person to a powerful idea. Research has confirmed the common sense that some beliefs held by an individual are more important than others. By important here is meant a belief which when changed causes a great number of changes throughout the rest of the belief system. These powerful beliefs will be called nuclear because they are at the heart of a person's belief system. Change within a person's value system is most possible when these nuclear beliefs are changed and they in turn cause a chain reaction throughout the rest of the system. To some extent, persons differ in what they consider most important. Hence not everyone has the same nuclear beliefs. But deep within the personality, practically all individuals are very much concerned with those persons who are significant in their lives, who give them signs of appreciation and a positive evaluation. This in part explains why a change in a person's value system is best accomplished when the individual is attracted to someone who embodies Christian values and who tells the youth he or she has great potential and self-worth. This is how social and psychological factors can function together in cooperation with the work of the Holy Spirit to foster growth in values.

The surveys with which this book began described the inadequacy and strain many parents felt in their communication with their children. Indications were that as many as two-thirds of the parents had these problems. But these studies ought not to be taken literally although the problem to which they point is real enough. The parents' statements about their feelings must be taken as accurately reflecting what they in fact do feel. But the parents' statements may not be giving a fair picture of the total situation. Their relationships with their children may rest on a much more solid basis than the parents realize. The reasons for saying this will be explained in the concluding chapter.

CHAPTER SEVEN: Moral Development through the Sharing of Symbols

This book began with a description of changes which have occurred in the way many of today's parents and children understand authority as it operates in the home, school, and church. One central idea was proposed throughout the chapters: the most effective way for parents to share their Christian values is by helping their children develop the ability to recognize and balance the various value tensions behind these changes and events within our society.

Chapter one described three fundamental tensions which are at the root of the value changes within society. Those three tensions were identified as being between community and individual, content and process in education, and authoritarian versus nonauthoritarian emphases. Those sets of tensions are typically portrayed as opposites. But here they have been given as examples of tensions which need to be clearly understood and delicately balanced if values are to properly develop. Youth need to first recognize the value inherent in each side of the controversy. Then, eventually, they need to develop the ability to see that the values are not opposites but complementary emphases, each having its proper time and place.

Chapter two then explained selected religious and psychological implications of the three terms: "personal," "moral," and "development." It was proposed that the development of responsible moral values, although certainly influenced by environment, strongly depends on the youngster's mental and emotional maturity. Further, it was explained that values are beliefs which are put into action. The values are not authentic values unless the good will becomes translated into actions. In that context, it was further explained that moral values can not be simply taught from the outside but must develop from within.

Chapters three through six then gave an analysis of selected factors which impact on value formation during the preschool, middle, junior and senior high years respectively. The same theme was reiterated. Tensions, properly handled, can actually foster human and religious values. Development requires the balancing of different pulls such as wanting to conform to peers but also wanting to be independent from the group. No attempt was made to give an in-depth description of what parents should do, practically speaking, from day to day or year to year. Rather, the guiding conviction behind this book has been that the most practical approach for parents is a solid theory. A clearly understood theory as to how parents can guide their children's moral development provides a consistency which a bundle of techniques alone can not.

How does the theory here presented compare with those espoused by authors who have been so widely read by parents and religious educators during recent years? A concise restatement of the present theme will help broaden the discussion. Youth develop moral values when they are challenged to develop these values. The best way to challenge them is by helping them to have experiences which let them see alternatives and the consequences of each alternative. The youth must first see the need for developing positive Christian values and commitments. Otherwise, they will travel the path of least resistance and care only about their own personal needs.

How then does this approach compare with other substantive approaches to value formation? Each theory and author has a particular perspective and peculiar vocabulary. But, what is basic to each of these approaches is the conviction that authentic values develop only through the experience of dialectic or pulls toward seemingly opposite values. Lawrence Kohlberg of Harvard has a theory which is widely used in both public and religious schools. He has identified six ways of understanding justice. He generalizes those into six types of moral reasoning ranging from the young child's standard of reward and punishment to the adult's mature altruism. He also found that the shift from an earlier to a later stage of reasoning takes years to develop and can not be rushed by any techniques. When the de-

velopment does occur, Kohlberg found, it happens through the person's having become aware of "dissonance" or a clash of values. The person becomes dissatisfied with previous values and is attracted to a more complex understanding.

This type of finding is one reason why the approach taken in this book has emphasized that moral growth has two phases. First, there is the recognition of a tension such as between what is and what could or should be. What then follows is the resolution of that tension. For example, the early adolescent, happy in his belonging to the peer group, first begins to feel its domination and then attempts to work out the balance between belonging and domination. The underlying dynamic inherent in Kohlberg's popular dilemma-solving approach to fostering moral development has much broader implications than has been generally recognized by the grassroots educators. There is a much broader principle beneath the now widespread classroom technique for furthering youth's understanding of justice. That principle is that all development, whether moral, social, or religious, comes through balancing the tensions which can be found in the situations of real life.

Other authors with whom parents may be more familiar also use this technique of balancing tensions. Haim Ginott, the psychologist whose *Between Parent and Child* and *Between Parent and Teenager* have touched well over a million readers, teaches an approach which consists of examples of how to solve various problems. He teaches parents, for example, how to point out problems without criticizing, how to express anger without insulting, and how to offer praise without evaluating. Such helpful techniques, once again, are simply examples of the fundamental approach of gaining better insights and then balancing what initially may seem to be opposite values.

Also widely used by parents and teachers has been Thomas Gordon's no-lose method of parent effectiveness training. His six steps for resolving problems are once again helpful techniques for balancing opposites, particularly the "authority" of both the child and the adult. This in turn leads to sorting out respective responsibilities, to raising alternative solutions, and then to finding out which alternative works best in particular situations.

The beauty and grace of this method is that it enables the family to focus on the problem and its solutions. It keeps the attention away from personal issues, so there is less need for defensiveness and for aggressively bringing up the past faults of family members. This focus is quite instructive for it gives parents further clarification on how they can help their children develop moral values. Gordon's no-lose method gives adults and youth "distance," or room to breathe. It gives them a method which, when learned, becomes a ritual which gives permission to imagine new solutions to old problems. This method has more to do with a Christian approach to values than may at first be apparent.

The Mystery of Persons

There is a subtle dynamic at work in these various approaches to helping parents and children negotiate their differences. The dynamic is not at all foreign to Christian morality. Simply put, this dynamic consists in respecting the mystery of each person and avoiding the stereotyping of family members. A brief explanation of what it means to "avoid stereotyping individuals" will serve to underscore what it means to say a person is a mystery. And it will also serve as an example of how the theme of this book, development through balancing tensions, is implied in the Christian belief in the sacred mystery of the individual.

Throughout the history of Christianity, theologians and pious believers alike have tried to answer the question: Who is God? The more profound theologians such as Thomas Aquinas in the thirteenth century and Karl Rahner in the twentieth have consistently affirmed that God is a mystery. By this they mean that God is so transcendent that the one attribute man can most surely use to describe him is his incomprehensibility. Language, being finite, necessarily falls short of describing the infinite.

The way the great theological traditions have handled this question is by using paradox. They say God is both far and near, both transcendent and immanent. He dwells in the farthest heavens and yet in each person's heart. This is how Christianity balances the tension concerning its most basic question: Who is God? To think that God is simply that person who is portrayed in various Old and New Testament stories would be to stereotype divinity and to lose hold of the tension. God is as the Scriptures give witness, but he is much more than those individual stories suggest.

This theological approach to the mystery of God is instructive as an illustration of how parents can approach moral values, namely, through the mystery of the person. The person is much more than previous experiences or present problems suggest he or she is. This conviction needs to be foremost within the Christian family.

There are three principles which exemplify how parents can help their children develop this strong sense of the mystery of person. They are adaptations of family therapist Murray Bowen's approach to counseling the family as though it were an emotional system.

1) Accent the child's individuality. The child who receives a letter or package addressed to him, brought by the postman, is as excited as any child on Christmas morning. This is not simply greed but rather the joy of knowing that someone "out there" is thinking of the child, offering a surprise, and talking directly to the child. Moral values are best shared through such interpersonal intimacies.

2) Present the child with an image of a strong parent who takes responsibility for what he or she says. For example, the parent who wants the child to do something should begin the sentence with "I want." Other statements such as "we ought" or "you ought to do such and such" can be indicative of an unwillingness to accept authority and responsibility. The concern here is for the attitude and principles that are conveyed by the words. The child that implicitly understands responsibility and can say "I did this" or "I need that" has taken an important step toward developing a personal value system. Only an "I" can respond to the needs of others.

3) Be supportive and affectionate rather than dominating. Children best develop the ability to love if their environment is loving and their parents are expressive toward each other. The child who has many ways of expressing affection will have little need for absolutizing a materialistic approach to showing love for others.

This concluding chapter has thus far considered how the theme of balancing tensions is integral to many contemporary methods for parents to share values with their children. Priority has been given to the mystery of the person and how that is consistent with the Christian understanding of morality as described in Chapter two. This mystery of the person is what today's teachers need to keep front and center as they attempt to utilize Kohlberg's stage-theory approach to moral development. It is so easy for the teacher to lose sight of the child amid the characteristics of the stages. This results in the child being categorized and stereotyped.

One final consideration summarizes much of what has been discussed and provides common ground between the findings of contemporary research and the values of Christian tradition. Sociologist Stephen Wieting compared the religious beliefs and practices of parents with those of their children. He concluded that the two generations at first gave the impression that parents and children had widely separate religious beliefs. But Wieting suggests that the two generations were using different vocabularies but their values were probably closer together than either group realized. This is important when considering the finding with which this book began, that two-thirds of the parents tested had difficulty talking with their children concerning matters of importance. Wieting further suggests that one way to share religious values and to reduce conflict in the family would be for parents and children to emphasize the symbolic rather than the literal aspects of their faith. Practically speaking, this means the family members would do well to share with each other their appreciation and insights of what various religious beliefs mean to them. This can be challenging to each person's understanding. It can provide a healthy tension. The members would not dogmatize any one interpretation of a belief or doctrine in an authoritarian manner. Such a literal approach would reduce the religious belief's rich meanings to a single verbalization or statement.

The characteristics of a symbol are that it moves a person deeply, taps the riches of the memory, stretches the imagination, and allows the person to consider a number of implications. A powerful symbol draws on the strengths of both emotion and intellect, on affection and understanding. So this symbolic approach to interpreting beliefs is also being recommended for interpreting the actions of family members. When the child does something that might displease the parents, this approach would invite parents to ask the youth to explain what they saw happen to the things and persons involved and also why the child did that particular action. So what this book has been emphasizing is that "accountability" is what the children need to be trained in if the parents are going to effectively guide the child's moral development. Such parent-child discussions can be painstakingly slow and certainly require considerably more effort and time than simply giving a command or a swat. But the long-term reward promises to be a young adult, who, with God's help and man's cooperation, will be capable of making responsible moral decisions and contributing to the needs of the Christian and broader human communities.

Suggestions for Further Reading

**Fostering Moral Development
in Today's Family** (Chapter One)

Bronfenbrenner, Urie. *Two Worlds of Childhood.*
   New York: Russell Sage Foundation, 1970.
Erikson, Erik. *Childhood and Society.* New York:
   W.W. Norton, Inc., 1963.
Paradis, Wilfrid H., and Thompson, Andrew D.
   Where are the 6.6 Million? Washington, DC:
   United States Catholic Conference, 1976.
Rokeach, Milton. *The Open and Closed Mind.* New
   York: Basic Books, Inc., 1960.
Yankelovich, Skelly, and White Inc. *General Mills
   American Family Report, 1976-77, Raising Chil-
   dren in a Changing Society.* New York: General
   Mills, Inc., 1977.

The Meaning of Personal Moral Development (Chapter Two)

Bornkaam, Günther. *Jesus of Nazareth.* New York: Harper and Row, 1960.

Curran, Charles. *Christian Morality Today: The Renewal of Moral Theology.* Notre Dame, IN: Fides/Claretian Publishers, 1966.

Damon, William. *The Social World of the Child.* San Francisco: Jossey-Bass Publishers, 1977.

Depalma, D., and Foley, J., ed. *Moral Development: Current Theory and Research.* Hillsdale, NJ: Lawrence Erlbaum Associates, 1975.

Dulles, Avery. *The Survival of Dogma: Faith, Authority and Dogma in a Changing World.* Garden City: Doubleday, 1973.

Duska, Ronald, and Whelan, Mariellen. *Moral Development: A Guide to Piaget and Kohlberg.* New York: Paulist Press, 1975.

Fowler, James. "Religious Insititutions: Toward a Developmental Perspective on Faith." *Religious Education* Vol. 69, March-April, 1974.

Greeley, Andrew. *The Jesus Myth.* Garden City: Doubleday, 1971.

Kohlberg, Lawrence. "The Study of Moral Development," In *Moral Development and Behavior,* edited by T. Lickona. New York: Holt, Rinehart and Winston, 1976.

Simon, Sidney, *et al. Values and Teaching: Working with Values in the Classroom.* Columbus: Charles Merrill Publications, 1966.

Preschool and
Middle School Years (Chapters Three and Four)

Bettleheim, Bruno. *The Children of the Dream.* New York: Macmillan Company, 1969.

Brown, Roger, ed. *Cognitive Development in Childhood.* Chicago: University of Chicago Press, 1970.

Flavel, John H. *The Development of Role-Taking and Communication Skills in Children.* Huntington, New York: Robert E. Krieger Publishers, 1975.

Ginsburg, Herbert, and Opper, Sylvia. *Piaget's Theory of Intellectual Development.* Englewood Cliffs, NJ: Prentice-Hall Inc., 1969.

Goldman, Ronald. *Readiness for Religion: A Basis for Developmental Religious Education.* New York: Seabury Press, 1970.

Gordon, Ira J. *Baby Learning through Baby Play: A Parents' Guide to the First Two Years.* New York: St. Martin's Press, 1970.

Marthaler, Berard L. *Catechetics in Context.* Huntington, IN: Our Sunday Visitor Press, 1970.

Nelsen, Hart; Petvin, Raymond; and Shields, Joseph. *The Religion of Children.* Washington, DC: United States Catholic Conference, 1977.

Piaget, Jean. *The Psychology of the Child.* New York: Basic Books, Inc., 1969.

Strommen, Merton, ed. *Research on Religious Development.* New York: Hawthorn Books, Inc., 1971.

United States Catholic Conference. *Resources for Family Sacramental Celebration.* Washington, DC: USCC, 1976.

White, Burton L. *The First Three Years of Life.* Englewood Cliffs, NJ: Prentice-Hall, Inc., 1975.

Junior and Senior
High School Years (Chapters Five and Six)

Adelson, Joseph. "The Mystique of Adolescence." *Psychiatry* 1964.

Elkind, David, and Elkind, Sally. "Varieties of Religious Experience in the Young Adolescent." *Journal For the Scientific Study of Religion* II, Fall, 1962.

Fichter, Joseph. "Religion and Socialization Among Children." *Review of Religious Research* IV, Fall, 1962.

Friedenberg, Edgar. *The Vanishing Adolescent.* Boston: Beacon Press, 1959.

Gesell, Arnold. *Youth: The Years from Ten to Sixteen.* New York: Harper and Row, 1956.

Potvin, Raymond; Hoge, Dean; and Nelsen, Hart. *Religion and American Youth.* Washington, DC: United States Catholic Conference, 1976.

Rokeach, Milton. *The Nature of Human Values.* New York: Free Press, 1973.

_____. *Beliefs, Attitudes and Values.* San Francisco: Jossey-Bass Publishers, 1968.

Selman, R., and Bryne, D. "A Structural Analysis of Role-Taking Levels in Middle Childhood." *Child Development* 45, 1974.

Stewart, Charles William. *Adolescent Religion: A Developmental Study of the Religion of Youth.* Nashville: Abingdon Press, 1967.

Strommen, Merton. *A Study of Generations.* Minneapolis: Augsburg Publishing House, 1972.

_____. *Five Cries of Youth.* New York: Harper and Row, 1974.

Turiel, Eliot. "Conflicts and Transition in Adolescent Moral Development." *Child Development* 45, 1974.

Moral Development through
the Sharing of Symbols (Chapter Seven)

Bowen, Murray. "Principles and Techniques of Multiple Family Therapy." In *Systems Therapy,* edited by Jack Bradt. Washington, DC: Groome Child Guidance Center, 1971.

Fowler, James. "The Structural-Developmental Approach." In *Values and Moral Development,* edited by James Hennessy. New York: Paulist Press, 1976.

Ginott, Haim G. *Between Parent and Teenager.* New York: Macmillan Co., 1969.

_____. *Between Parent and Child.* New York: Macmillan Co., 1965.

Gordon, Thomas. *Parent Effectiveness Training.* New York: New American Library, 1975.

Kurtines, William, and Greif, Esther. "The Development of Moral Thought." *Psychological Bulletin* Vol. 81, Aug, 1974.

Saltzstein, Herbert D. "Social Development and Moral Development: A Perspective on the Role of Parents and Peers." In *Moral Development and Behavior,* edited by T. Lickona. New York: Holt, Rinehart and Winston, 1976.

Wieting, Stephen G. "An Examination of Intergenerational Patterns of Religious Belief and Practices." *Sociological Analysis: A Journal in the Sociology of Religion* Vol. 36, No. 2, 1975.

Youniss, James. "Another Perspective on Social Cognition." In *Minnesota Symposia on Child Psychology, Vol. 9,* edited by A. Pick. Minneapolis: University of Minnesota Press, 1975.